How To Tell When You're Really Old!

Funny Happens When Kids Define Old Age

Kristi Porter

CONTENTS

Dedication   2

The Story Behind This Book   3

Part I   5

Part II   16

Part III   27

A Note From The Author   38

Other Books by Kristi Porter   39

About the Author   40

Connect With Kristi Online   40

Acknowledgements   41

Dedication

This book is dedicated to every parent, grandparent, and caregiver that entrusted me with the care and education of their child over the years.

We've all earned a good laugh.

And to the Happi Kamper Kids, the preschoolers at Community United Methodist Preschool, and the Power Play Kids, who all had a part in providing me with material for this book.

Keep smiling and providing those laughs!

The Story Behind This Book

How To Tell When You're Really Old! is the result of hundreds of interviews with young children ages three to twelve, who were simply asked how they could tell when someone was old, and allowed to answer freely, giving as much or as little explanation as they saw fit.

It began as part of a larger class project by teacher Kristi Porter and the children of Happi Kamper Child Care, located in North Muskegon, Michigan. Each child was to create an individual gift book for his or her parents, and *How To Tell When You're Really Old!* was simply to be one chapter in each child's book.

Now, the individual answers of the Happi Kamper Kids, as well as those of the children at Community United Methodist Preschool, and the kids of Power Play Childcare have been combined. Their diverse, candid, and uncensored answers may surprise you, or even make you laugh out loud, as you get a quick glimpse into the amazing and intricate minds of some of the most delightful and fascinating children around. Enjoy!

PART I

… Old people wear fancy clothes and watch boring TV in the day and old movies at night. They also like to play a little bit of football - just a little bit though - then they have to go to bed. Except my Nana, she's like 80 so she doesn't play football anymore; I think she's the referee. ~Denny, age 5.

~ * ~ * ~ * ~ * ~ * ~ * ~

… When you are old you look kinda silly and put all your hair under a funny hat. You can't put your face under a hat though! ~Lindy, age 4.

~ * ~ * ~ * ~ * ~ * ~ * ~

… Old people know a lot about numbers. And they can cook new things and read books, too. But their best thing is when they talk on the phone to little kids. They really like that! ~William G., age 5.

~ * ~ * ~ * ~ * ~ * ~ * ~

…Old people can draw with markers all by themselves, and sometimes they can even cook breakfast. They can't play ring-around-the-rosy or pop-goes-the-weasel, though. But they can roll over really good! ~Isabelle R., age 4.

~ * ~ * ~ * ~ * ~ * ~ * ~

5

... You might be old if you look like you are married, and that's not good. Lots of old people look kinda like dinosaurs; well, at least some of them do. ~Hunter N., age 4.

~ * ~ * ~ * ~ * ~ * ~ * ~

... Old people don't like to play anymore, so they just die. But I'm not really sure though, 'cause I don't know any old people. Maybe they all died. ~ Dylan S., age 4.

~ * ~ * ~ * ~ * ~ * ~ * ~

... If you are old you have to like having stripes on your face, and wearing glasses and dresses all the time. 'Cept old boy people, they just wear pants with no socks. ~Nick R., age 4.

~ * ~ * ~ * ~ * ~ * ~ * ~

... Old people just wear underwear to bed - like my dad. And they eat roast beef meat and can saw wood with real saws. They also like to go to the grocery store, but mostly they just stay in their bedroom and sleep. ~Brett, age 4.

~ * ~ * ~ * ~ * ~ * ~ * ~

... Old people have melty faces, so they just pretty much stay home with their dogs. ~Sydney E., age 5.

~ * ~ * ~ * ~ * ~ * ~ * ~

... My grandma is really, *really* old – like 18 or something. She just stays home and watches TV and sings the Annie song. Sometimes she goes to see the other old people though, and they all eat pickles and oranges at the table. ~Shayna, age 3.

~ * ~ * ~ * ~ * ~ * ~ * ~

... I like old people. They know how to draw good "e'"s. ~Maddie, age 3.

~ * ~ * ~ * ~ * ~ * ~ * ~

... Old people are crabby, and snore when they sleep. Some old ladies just wear pajamas all day. But old grandpas have to wear underwear and stay in the bedroom - they're not allowed in the living room. ~Jennifer, age 3.

~ * ~ * ~ * ~ * ~ * ~ * ~

… All I know about old people is that they are both grouchy and nice -- but not on the same day. ~Spencer, age 4.

~ * ~ * ~ * ~ * ~ * ~ * ~

… Old people pretty much speak like, well, not like a real human. And their skin is very wrinkly so they just have to sit around all day and watch TV, like my poppa. ~Devin, age 8.

~ * ~ * ~ * ~ * ~ * ~ * ~

… You are old when you have ugly cracks on your feet. Old people get really cold sometimes if they go outside, so some of them just hang around at home or go somewhere warm - like California - unless they don't know where that is. Then they just use lots of blankets. ~Hunter C., age 4.

~ * ~ * ~ * ~ * ~ * ~ * ~

… Old people have a face that is kinda crumbly. They live in really old houses and wash their hands a lot, but they do go to Chuckie Cheese's and help kids play games sometimes. But then they have to go home and do really hard work – like making paper. Then they die. ~Alec, age 4.

~ * ~ * ~ * ~ * ~ * ~ * ~

… Did you know that old people can get even older than dogs and cats? That's probably why they scream when they look in the mirror. ~Lynn, age 4.

~ * ~ * ~ * ~ * ~ * ~ * ~

7

… Old people look like a grandpa, or my dad. When you're really old you have a different home and you get a new color hair. Really old people get bigger and nicer, and they can cook stuff. But they only have a few pans. You are really old when you are 160. ~Charles, age 5.

~ * ~ * ~ * ~ * ~ * ~ * ~

… When you grow up to be old your skin is "movey" and your hair is gray. Most old people eat garlic and onions and other yucky stuff that's good for them, but they don't have any fun. They just sit around in the rest home and look at the other old people. ~Julia A., age 4.

~ * ~ * ~ * ~ * ~ * ~ * ~

… You know you are old when your name is grandma and you are very wrinkly. Old people wear too much make-up and most of their hair falls out. Sometimes they yell at people, too. Really old people only eat salads and then worry about their health. You are really old when you are 50. ~AJ, age 11.

~ * ~ * ~ * ~ * ~ * ~ * ~

… Old people are kinda chunky and usually very tired. When you are old you have red spots on your arms, and like to go to stores. That's all I know about old people. ~Jennie, age 4.

~ * ~ * ~ * ~ * ~ * ~ * ~

… Really old people look like they have glue on their face, so they put on lots of make-up - but it doesn't help. On the weekend they go and walk around in stores. But usually they just sit around and talk about pretend things. ~Reider, age 4.

~ * ~ * ~ * ~ * ~ * ~ * ~

… Old people have grandchildren and like to dance to old music. Really old ladies can't have babies, but they can always adopt one if they want. The oldest person in the world is my great grandma, she's 89. ~Chloe, age 8.

~ * ~ * ~ * ~ * ~ * ~ * ~

… I only know a little bit about old people. I know they have a yard sale and sell all their stuff, and then a dump truck comes and puts them in it and takes them to heaven. And that's it. ~Delaney W., age 3.

~ * ~ * ~ * ~ * ~ * ~ * ~

… Old people only have hair on the sides of their head and have to wear old clothes. I think some of them like to live under big stones. They can go out in the daytime, but they have to go to concerts and sing songs at night. Then they eat lots of spinach and drink coffee until they die. That's when they are about 200, I think. ~Zachary M., age 4.

~ * ~ * ~ * ~ * ~ * ~ * ~

… Old people study a lot, but I don't know why. Really old people look silly 'cause they wear funny clothes, and I think that's why they have to live far, far away. ~Olivia W., age 4.

~ * ~ * ~ * ~ * ~ * ~ * ~

… You know you are old when you are about 67, have age marks on your skin and lay down all day. Sometimes really old people like to play with their grandkids. And for some reason they actually like to clean the house - I don't get it. ~Ben H. age 7.

~ * ~ * ~ * ~ * ~ * ~ * ~

… Old people really don't do anything. They just buy stuff and eat food like lettuce and pickles. You are really old when you have more than 14 birthdays! ~Gus, age 4.

~ * ~ * ~ * ~ * ~ * ~ * ~

... Your face looks kinda like a brown circle when you are old. You can still go to the playground, but you have to just watch the little kids play, and when you get bored you can just go home and play on the computer. ~Noah, age 4.

~ * ~ * ~ * ~ * ~ * ~ * ~

... Old people are nice. They just sit in a rocking chair, watch TV, and share their cake with me. ~Rylee, age 4.

~ * ~ * ~ * ~ * ~ * ~ * ~

... Cat ladies are very old. They have a different kind of hair, and buy lots of bananas. They like to eat chicken and drink milk, and play with their cats every day. But they look kinda like a bear. ~Renee, age 3.

~ * ~ * ~ * ~ * ~ * ~ * ~

... Old people like to swim, and eat bananas and ice cream for dinner - but just vanilla- they don't like chocolate. Old people can't ever go outside so they just stay in their rooms to play; and sometimes they feed the little fishy in the bowl. ~Cami, age 4.

~ * ~ * ~ * ~ * ~ * ~ * ~

... Really old people look kinda funny, you know, like they're dead. They have to stay home and watch TV 'cause they are too old to go anywhere else. But other old people come over to play with them sometimes, so they are pretty happy. ~Grace L., age 3.

~ * ~ * ~ * ~ * ~ * ~ * ~

... You have gray hair when you get old. Some old people live with little kids, but most of them don't. They just sit home, watch the news and eat with dentures, you know - pretend teeth. And they like to go bowling on Saturday. That's pretty much all I know, 'cept you turn old when you are maybe 49 or something like that. ~Joseph N., age 5.

~ * ~ * ~ * ~ * ~ * ~ * ~

...Lots of old people go to restaurants and stores, but really old people go to heaven to be angels. ~Kayla M., age 4.

~ * ~ * ~ * ~ * ~ * ~ * ~

... Old people are 65. They wear nice clothes and go to the Disney On Ice show. Really old people watch TV every day and make good banana bread and cookies. They also like to go shopping and buy kids stuff. ~Emilia, age 4.

~ * ~ * ~ * ~ * ~ * ~ * ~

... Sometimes old people are allowed to go to the store without their kids. But usually they only go to lots of doctors 'cause they get sick a lot. Really old people have a *lot* of birthdays. ~Garrett, age 4.

~ * ~ * ~ * ~ * ~ * ~ * ~

... Old people look skinny, and are usually grumpy because they have to wear ugly clothes. ~Jake H., age 4.

~ * ~ * ~ * ~ * ~ * ~ * ~

... I think old people should not be allowed to eat soup, 'cause it just spills on their chin and then they are grouchy all day. Maybe they need to get dressed, 'cause usually they just wear pajamas instead of clothes. ~Meagan, age 4.

~ * ~ * ~ * ~ * ~ * ~ * ~

... When you wear glasses and look like my grandma, you are old. Really old people like to watch TV all day and play with grown up cars. They like to go shopping too. ~Ansley, age 4.

~ * ~ * ~ * ~ * ~ * ~ * ~

... You are old when you are 100 and when you drink some water you have to pee a lot. Oh, and you might have to walk on crutches too if you don't want to sit down. ~Haley, age 4.

~ * ~ * ~ * ~ * ~ * ~ * ~

... Really old people get kinda blond hair, are really nice, and give kids lots of hugs. I like old people. ~Erin, age 3.

~ * ~ * ~ * ~ * ~ * ~ * ~

... When someone gets to 20 they are really old. Then they can eat macaroni every day and live in a purple house if they want to. They don't have to go to school, and can stay home and watch TV and just have fun all day. ~Josie E., age 4.

~ * ~ * ~ * ~ * ~ * ~ * ~

... Old people eat chicken and drink beer every day. Then they just comb their hair and go to sleep. ~Tommy, age 3.

~ * ~ * ~ * ~ * ~ * ~ * ~

... Really old people eat grapes and bananas, and like to play the hungry cats game. They get sick a lot so they have to eat fruit snacks and wash their hands with soap. Really old people laugh a lot and are pretty happy – but I don't know why. ~Brenden M., age 3.

~ * ~ * ~ * ~ * ~ * ~ * ~

... You know you're old when you look kinda like a big circle with a head. Old people always clean stuff and buy dolls and draw nice pictures. They love little kids, too. ~Clare, age 3.

~ * ~ * ~ * ~ * ~ * ~ * ~

... If you are 99, you are old and can go outside with no shirt on whenever you want. But you probably can't walk very good when you are that old. You will talk a little bit funny, too. Some old people are teachers, but if you're really, really old then you just stay home and watch TV. ~Kaleb, age 5.

~ * ~ * ~ * ~ * ~ * ~ * ~

… Old people have mustaches. My dad is almost old, 'cause he's growing a mustache; but my mom's not, so she's not old yet. ~Troy O., age 5.

~ * ~ * ~ * ~ * ~ * ~ * ~

… Old people look like my mom. They only eat, clean, and do yucky stuff. They don't get to have fun. ~Katie C., age 4.

~ * ~ * ~ * ~ * ~ * ~ * ~

… You get old when you are like 11 years old I think. Then you get a new body that is an old one, and do the laundry for fun. But you get to eat whatever you want and go to bed late, so that's pretty cool. ~Ashley R., age 4.

~ * ~ * ~ * ~ * ~ * ~ * ~

… Some old people go to heaven. All the others ones go to Canada. ~Matthew, age 4.

~ * ~ * ~ * ~ * ~ * ~ * ~

… When you get old you usually break your leg, or you get a fever, or you have a sliver in your toe or something. Then you have to go to the doctor. Really old people need a lot of medicine to make them better. Then they can play with their animal toys again. ~Colin, age 4.

~ * ~ * ~ * ~ * ~ * ~ * ~

… Old people like to push kids on the swings, but they do it very gentle. They also go swimming - but they have to wear a swimming jacket so they don't sink. Then they go home and eat sandwiches and milkshakes and do some dancing before they die. ~Allison, age 4.

~ * ~ * ~ * ~ * ~ * ~ * ~

13

… Old people usually look grumpy all the time so they have to go on vacations a lot. But when you're 37 like my dad you are not really old yet, but almost old. ~Evan, age 4.

~ * ~ * ~ * ~ * ~ * ~ * ~

… Really old people are grouchy a lot and nice a little. They dress up like clowns to go shopping, and then they eat steak and make the kids stay in their bedroom. ~Emma T., age 4.

~ * ~ * ~ * ~ * ~ * ~ * ~

… If you are 10½, you are pretty old and can order pizza and make potatoes by yourself. Old people babysit kids for fun, and they even do it for free. I think old people are very nice, even if they do look all wrinkly and stuff. ~Makenna, age 4

~ * ~ * ~ * ~ * ~ * ~ * ~

… Fifty is when somebody gets really old. That's when they start to look gross and eat a lot of vegetables and fruit and other healthy food. Old people like to clean things a lot, and always live in old houses on bumpy roads. ~Kenzie, age 4.

~ * ~ * ~ * ~ * ~ * ~ * ~

… Really old people look ugly 'cause they get brown spots on them. They like to work on houses sometimes, and kinda like to play around - but not too much 'cause they might get sick and die. Mostly old people like to look for dinosaur bones. ~Trevor, age 4.

~ * ~ * ~ * ~ * ~ * ~ * ~

… Teachers are really old. So are grandmas and grandpas. Old people are mean sometimes because they are only allowed to play with octagon toys and bears; so they usually live far, far away and take lots of naps. ~Lily H., age 3.

~ * ~ * ~ * ~ * ~ * ~ * ~

…Old people can't have any more fun. They just have to babysit kids and watch TV all day. ~Gwendolyn, age 4.

~ * ~ * ~ * ~ * ~ * ~ * ~

... Really old people have to blow out a lot of candles. Then they turn red all over and have to lay down and look at rainbows. ~Morgan, age 3.

~ * ~ * ~ * ~ * ~ * ~ * ~

... When you have two colors in your hair, like brown and white, you are about 40 – and that means you're old. Then you look like a grandma or grandpa, live in a new house and cook stuff like spaghetti, or maybe a little bit of pancakes. Then you go in the living room and rest. ~Shelby, age 4.

~ * ~ * ~ * ~ * ~ * ~ * ~

... Well, old people look kinda mean, and have red hair and weird clothes. They usually eat stuff that kids don't like - so then they die and go live in heaven. ~Collyn, age 4.

~ * ~ * ~ * ~ * ~ * ~ * ~

... If you have funny skin that kinda sticks out and grow hair on your chin, then you're probably old. Really old people are about 60, I think. They like to eat chicken for dinner, and then they walk slow to the church and sit down, and then they just wait there until they go to heaven. ~Dallas, age 4.

~ * ~ * ~ * ~ * ~ * ~ * ~

... I think really old people used to be human but then one day they wake up old, you know, with scrunched up faces and stuff. They have to walk slow and never run. They just stand around and look at stuff and drink wine. And sometimes they eat ham. ~Brennan, age 4.

~ * ~ * ~ * ~ * ~ * ~ * ~

PART II

... When you get to be really old you need a thing-a-ma-bobber to help you walk, and you don't have any teeth so you just chew stuff with your lips. Sometimes old people like to snowblow with their snowblowers, but they don't really like it if you throw snowballs at them. ~Landon, age 5.

~ * ~ * ~ * ~ * ~ * ~ * ~

... Old people are 60. Really old people look sick a lot and they have a stick to help them walk. But mostly they just like to wait around – like for something to eat. Old people have lots of keys to open things, but they usually live in the hospital and just lay there. ~Adam, age 3.

~ * ~ * ~ * ~ * ~ * ~ * ~

... If you look like Debbie that goes to my church, you are pretty old. Really, really old people live far away and have to go to the doctor once a week. They eat lots of carrots to make them healthy so they can sit around and watch TV. Old people are usually more than 42. ~Isabelle L., age 5.

~ * ~ * ~ * ~ * ~ * ~ * ~

... Old people have messy hair and smile a lot. They go to church a lot, too. Then they take all their clothes off and sit in the hot tub. After that they like to watch the super bowl on TV. ~Wesley, age 5.

~ * ~ * ~ * ~ * ~ * ~ * ~

… Old people are grouchy and read newspapers all day. They have to walk really, really slow and never, ever play video games. But mostly the way you can tell if somebody is old is if hair comes out of their nose! ~Mason, age 4.

~ * ~ * ~ * ~ * ~ * ~ * ~

… Wrinkled up faces and hands means you're old. Most old people just clean up around the house and then sit down and watch their shows. They don't have much fun – but they do go out and walk around the block sometimes. ~Alex, age 5.

~ * ~ * ~ * ~ * ~ * ~ * ~

… Some old people like to take children to McDonald's, but they only eat the food that the children don't like. The other old people stay home and do things that kids are not allowed to do. And sometimes old people even touch things that kids aren't allowed to touch. ~William A., age 4.

~ * ~ * ~ * ~ * ~ * ~ * ~

… You know you're really old when you hit your 40's. You look like my grandpa with a Hawkmo haircut – you know what that is right? Kinda like a reverse Mohawk. Then you get all wrinkly, have false teeth, and you start shrinking. Mostly old people play Bingo, but they sleep a lot and have to move a lot slower too. They also smell like prunes sometimes. I think that means they're going to die. ~Dennis, age 12.

~ * ~ * ~ * ~ * ~ * ~ * ~

… Old people don't have any hair, and have lots of brown spots and bloody spots on their skin, and eat pasta and wheat bread and then go to Michigan Adventures Park. But they just sit around - they can't go on the rides. ~Dylan D., age 4.

~ * ~ * ~ * ~ * ~ * ~ * ~

... You're old when your kids are grown up and in high school and you have grandchildren. When you're really old you have gray hair, your face gets wrinkled and you've done a job for a long, long time. You have a cane to walk and you are grumpy. Really old people can't drink anymore, so they go to the doctor a lot. They also have lots of cats and a dog. You are really old when you are 102. ~Dominique, age 8.

~ * ~ * ~ * ~ * ~ * ~ * ~

... Really old people only eat carrots, and have to work at stores 'cause they're not allowed to go anywhere else by themselves. ~Meagan, age 4.

~ * ~ * ~ * ~ * ~ * ~ * ~

... You know you're really old when you wear stupid clothes, get dentures, and your hair goes gray. Old people have skin that gets all wrinkly, and they can only eat soft food and have to live in an old folks home. Old people are very slow, and they always use wheelchairs and walkers. You are really old when you turn 40. ~Andy, age 10.

~ * ~ * ~ * ~ * ~ * ~ * ~

... Old people have skin that is like skinny and fat at the same time. They have white hair and sleep all day, except when they watch TV. My dad sleeps all day but his skin isn't skinny and fat, so I don't think he's too old yet. ~Jakob, age 4.

~ * ~ * ~ * ~ * ~ * ~ * ~

... You look kinda like a sad monster when you are old. Old people have to go live with nice monsters and then they get a nice bracelet and can ride a bicycle that looks like a chair. ~Noa E., age 3.

~ * ~ * ~ * ~ * ~ * ~ * ~

… Old people drink coffee and lots of milk. Sometimes they like to go for a drive and go shopping. And they eat chicken - 'cause old people *really* like chicken. ~Brenden N., age 4.

~ * ~ * ~ * ~ * ~ * ~ * ~

… When your legs get broke and you have to sit in a wheelchair you are old. Then you get a really old face and then you die. ~Jaegar, age 4.

~ * ~ * ~ * ~ * ~ * ~ * ~

… Really old people look tired and like to visit graveyards. But they have to be careful because if they fall asleep there, they will get dead, too. ~Michelle, age 5.

~ * ~ * ~ * ~ * ~ * ~ * ~

… If you are 5 years old and a mommy and a daddy, you can be old. Then you get to watch Scooby Doo all the time, and make good pictures like my grandma. ~Anthony H., age 3.

~ * ~ * ~ * ~ * ~ * ~ * ~

… Old people look like they're dead even when they're not. They don't eat very much - they just like to buy groceries and put them away. Then they use a big potty chair and go to bed, but not to sleep. They have to stay awake all night and watch TV. ~Jezica, age 4.

~ * ~ * ~ * ~ * ~ * ~ * ~

… Really old people look like my dad. When you are really old you don't get to eat at the table, you have to go eat outside, and it's your job to kill the spider in the bedroom.

You are really old when you are about 300, I think.
~Elizabeth, age 3.

~ * ~ * ~ * ~ * ~ * ~ * ~

… Old people grow up and get married. Then they start to walk hunched over and sit funny in chairs. Pretty soon their hair turns all white, and then they go and live in heaven.
~Emily E., age 4.

~ * ~ * ~ * ~ * ~ * ~ * ~

… Old people have to go to the doctor every week. Really old people go around in a wheelchair, laugh at little kids, and say funny things. Old people also like yucky stuff like pork and pickles. When they get too tired, they go live in heaven.
~Benjamin S., age 4.

~ * ~ * ~ * ~ * ~ * ~ * ~

… The oldest person I know is Verna, or maybe Edna. Verna is probably 80 I think, but Edna is about 90 so she's pretty much older. When you get that old you have wrinkly skin and fall down a lot, so you have to get a cane. And eat lots of oatmeal. ~Joseph Y., age 6.

~ * ~ * ~ * ~ * ~ * ~ * ~

… If someone calls you grandma or grandpa you are probably old. Regular old people play with puzzles. Really old people go on vacation. ~Emma W., age 3.

~ * ~ * ~ * ~ * ~ * ~ * ~

… Really old people look like my daddy and only wear t-shirts and sweatpants. They have kinda blond hair and have to go to work. Then they eat a tuna fish sandwich for lunch, and then they can go home and take a nap. ~Olivia R., age 4.

~ * ~ * ~ * ~ * ~ * ~ * ~

… Old people look like they have scratches and little lines all over their face and have white hair. Really old people forget a lot of stuff – like if I'm coming to visit. But they do remember to wear different shoes when they eat popcorn, and to wear old clothes with sleeves when they go in the woods. Old people are pretty nice when they're not sleeping. ~Ethan P., age 3.

~ * ~ * ~ * ~ * ~ * ~ * ~

… People that sit in a rolling chair are old, like 21, or maybe 25. They live in a cottage with other old people and eat just soup until they die, then they go to heaven. ~Natalie, age 4.

~ * ~ * ~ * ~ * ~ * ~ * ~

… When you are old you get black and white hair and you can't play with toys anymore. You just have to work on papers. Then you can go home and relax. ~Ashley S., age 4.

~ * ~ * ~ * ~ * ~ * ~ * ~

… Your dad tells you when you're getting old. Or you can know it if you crash your car, 'cause old people crash a lot - so some of them just stay home and wash the sink all day. ~Joe, age 3.

~ * ~ * ~ * ~ * ~ * ~ * ~

… When you get really old your belly button gets pretty icky and then you don't have one anymore. But you do get a cool thing to walk with though! ~Madison C., age 4.

~ * ~ * ~ * ~ * ~ * ~ * ~

… Old people eat cauliflower and wear old clothes. Really old people go to Africa and India and the other people miss them. Really, really, really old people look like a giraffe. If you want to know anything else, I think you need to ask my dad about it, 'cause he's pretty old. ~Chase, age 4.

~ * ~ * ~ * ~ * ~ * ~ * ~

… If you get too old you will look like you don't have the same skin, 'cause it turns kinda light white. Then you get taken away to old people jail and have to eat yucky food like grass and dirt. ~Riley, age 4.

~ * ~ * ~ * ~ * ~ * ~ * ~

… Old people are shaped a little bit different. Sometimes they like to play with rocket ships and little kids, but when they are home they just cook lunch and look at their old hair and ugly bodies in the mirror. ~Caleb R., age 4.

~ * ~ * ~ * ~ * ~ * ~ * ~

… You know somebody is really old when they die. But they live for a while first - like 20 years, I think. ~Kali, age 4.

~ * ~ * ~ * ~ * ~ * ~ * ~

… Old people can color with their grandchildren and stay in the lines. But they have to wear glasses so they can even see the lines. ~Gavin, age 5.

~ * ~ * ~ * ~ * ~ * ~ * ~

… People with a tangled face are pretty old. Their face gets all tangled up 'cause they do too many business calls and eat too much liver with gravy. Old people just need to sit in a chair and relax like my Grandpa Steve. He just watches TV and reads the paper all day. ~Samantha, age 4.

~ * ~ * ~ * ~ * ~ * ~ * ~

… I think you get old when you are about 16. Then you can go to a restaurant every day, but you still have to eat breakfast at home. Old people get old haircuts and drink lots of milk. They like to tell jokes to other old people so they will laugh. My dad is really old, I think he's probably 19. ~Stefan, age 4.

~ * ~ * ~ * ~ * ~ * ~ * ~

… Really old people are very sweet, and some of them wear glasses. They have wrinkly skin and gray or white hair. Some old people like to play tennis and wear cute skirts. Old people have to take a lot of pills to stay healthy. My aunt is the oldest person I know. She's 90. ~Paige, age 8.

~ * ~ * ~ * ~ * ~ * ~ * ~

… My grandma is really old, so if you are a lady you will probably look like her when you grow up. If you are a man, you will get yucky skin and live in a little old house when you get old. Old ladies like to sew, but old men just take naps, 'cause that's all they know how to do. ~Josie H., age 4.

~ * ~ * ~ * ~ * ~ * ~ * ~

… Old people go to the doctor for no reason - even when they're not sick! Then they just go swing on the swings with all the other old people. ~Fallon, age 3.

~ * ~ * ~ * ~ * ~ * ~ * ~

… Old people look usually like a mom or dad and like to sneak up on people. They usually live in a yellow house, take a bath with lots of bubbles, and like to play with trains - so they're pretty cool. ~Christian, age 4.

~ * ~ * ~ * ~ * ~ * ~ * ~

… When you look like my grandma, then you know you are getting old. Old people are allowed to go out to buy bagels, but then they have to go home and watch the news. ~Kayleigh, age 4.

~ * ~ * ~ * ~ * ~ * ~ * ~

… Old people usually wear pajamas all day, but they like to watch kids play - 'cause they can't remember how to play anymore. Then they just eat soup and taco meat, and drink beer and coffee all day long. ~Clark, age 5.

~ * ~ * ~ * ~ * ~ * ~ * ~

… Old people don't have very much fun. They get hurt a lot and have to lay down and watch TV – like my grandma. I think she's 46 or something, so she's pretty old. ~Sophia S., age 4.

~ * ~ * ~ * ~ * ~ * ~ * ~

… If you are a mommies's grandma, you are very old. Old people like to clean up the house, and for fun they take care of kids, or maybe play on the computer. They're only allowed to eat cheese and chicken, and they have to be kind to all the other old people. ~Grace T., age 4.

~ * ~ * ~ * ~ * ~ * ~ * ~

… Old people get bent, and then they die. ~Matt, age 4.

~ * ~ * ~ * ~ * ~ * ~ * ~

… I know all about old people because my grandma is really old, she's 86. When you first get old you get a bald head, your bones don't work like they used to, your teeth fall out, and you have heart trouble. Then, when you're really old, you need a cane and a hospital in case you fall down and break a hip. Really, really old people have hearts that beat like a long slow sound – kinda like "duuummmm" like that. And then they're dead. ~Korbin, age 9.

~ * ~ * ~ * ~ * ~ * ~ * ~

… Old people go to the store a lot, and they make silly faces and stick out their tongue when they eat yucky old people food. Sometimes they live in houses, but usually they live in castles until it's time to go to heaven. ~David T., age 4.

~ * ~ * ~ * ~ * ~ * ~ * ~

... Some old people have stick out hair, and some old people have down hair, but they stay at work in the day and go home at night so they don't know about it. ~Sydney T., age 3.

~ * ~ * ~ * ~ * ~ * ~ * ~

... A lot of old people get stupid when they are old and then they don't like anybody. They just want to play with their stuff, and go to the bar. But some of them live in cute houses, and they can even get married sometimes! ~Katie M., age 5.

~ * ~ * ~ * ~ * ~ * ~ * ~

... Old people are kinda like ghosts. They get old creaky-googly eyes and live at the nursing home where my dad works. Old people just drink stuff, not eat, because they don't have no teeth. And they lay in bed all day because they are so sick. I don't want to get old. ~Hunter S., age 3.

~ * ~ * ~ * ~ * ~ * ~ * ~

... Old people can't walk too good, and can't climb trees. They like to talk about heaven, live in purple houses, and eat chicken noodle soup - 'cause they get sick a *lot*. Old people like lots of hugs and to hold hands. Sometimes they even like to play with Play-dough. I love old people. ~Laura, age 3.

~ * ~ * ~ * ~ * ~ * ~ * ~

... Some old people are black, and some are white, but they all have purple spots on them. They get to stay home all by themselves and don't even need a babysitter! And they can even go shopping, or go out for coffee - if they can remember how to drive. ~Lorna, age 4.

~ * ~ * ~ * ~ * ~ * ~ * ~

… I think old people have to go to work because they are too slow to play. They can still go on vacation, but they have to eat broccoli, carrots, and mashed potatoes first. ~Julie, age 4.

~ * ~ * ~ * ~ * ~ * ~ * ~

… Old people just drink coffee and eat shrimp. That's it, that's all they do. ~Justine, age 5.

~ * ~ * ~ * ~ * ~ * ~ * ~

… When you are 40 you start to look kinda weird and are just a little bit old. When you are 80 you drink medicine instead of juice and are really, really old. When you are 100 you are not old anymore, 'cause you are dead. ~William L., age 6.

~ * ~ * ~ * ~ * ~ * ~ * ~

… Old people can live in a house in any state they want to. I know old people like to be babysitters and help teachers at school, but I think they like to cook all by themselves the most. ~Brielle, age 5.

~ * ~ * ~ * ~ * ~ * ~ * ~

… Old people do silly stuff – like wear pirate clothes when it isn't even Halloween. When they are about 200 years old they get dead sick and have to go live in heaven. ~Lily M., age 4.

~ * ~ * ~ * ~ * ~ * ~ * ~

… I'm used to being by old people, like my grandma and grandpa, so I'm not scared of them. Old people like to do all kinds of chores that their kids tell them about, but then they forget to do them. That's okay, 'cause they're gonna die pretty soon anyway. ~Rhiannon, age 4.

~ * ~ * ~ * ~ * ~ * ~ * ~

PART III

… Old people look like grown-ups and live in regular houses but change their names to grandma and grandpa so everybody knows they are old. ~Julia M., age 3.

~ * ~ * ~ * ~ * ~ * ~ * ~

… Usually old people like to eat just pancakes and water. And they have to sleep in a bed – not on a couch. ~Adrian, age 3.

~ * ~ * ~ * ~ * ~ * ~ * ~

… Old people usually look a little bit green and have purple kinda hair. They do lots of paperwork and talk on the phone and do silly dances. They also like to eat lots of apples and carrots - but only a little bit of macaroni. ~Allie, age 3.

~ * ~ * ~ * ~ * ~ * ~ * ~

… If old people look in the mirror they think they are dying, so they just wear old clothes and don't look in the mirror. ~Gracie, age 4.

~ * ~ * ~ * ~ * ~ * ~ * ~

… I think old people get worms inside their head somehow - so they have to live in the street, or maybe in old people houses, I'm not sure. They do like to go shopping once in a while, but mostly they just go to carnivals for fun. Except some old people - they just stay home. ~Hailey, age 4.

~ * ~ * ~ * ~ * ~ * ~ * ~

… Old people like to go in the pool and play with other old grown-ups. Then they go to the store and buy ice cream. But they still look sad because they don't want to be old, so they go home and play with their Barbie's. ~Noa W., age 4.

~ * ~ * ~ * ~ * ~ * ~ * ~

… All I know is old people get mad at you if you bite them. ~Mikey, age 3.

~ * ~ * ~ * ~ * ~ * ~ * ~

… Old people look like they have doggie hair, but they are very nice and love little kids. ~Olivia U., age 5.

~ * ~ * ~ * ~ * ~ * ~ * ~

… Really old people look all crusted up. They wear blue clothes all the time and like to play with kids. But usually they just stay home and eat meat pies all day – if they're not in heaven yet. ~Christopher, age 4.

~ * ~ * ~ * ~ * ~ * ~ * ~

… Old ladies never have any more babies, they just babysit kids and cats and dogs. Really old people act funny, lose a lot of teeth that don't ever grow back, and talk weird. Most old people are lazy – but not all of them though. Some of them have parakeets and kids that are grown-ups, or at least in high school. You are really old when you are about 100 years old. ~Chelsea, age 7.

~ * ~ * ~ * ~ * ~ * ~ * ~

… You are really old when you start to look kinda like a duck and wear Halloween stuff every day. ~Troy G., age 4.

~ * ~ * ~ * ~ * ~ * ~ * ~

… My mommy looks really old when she sleeps in her bed, but when she wakes ups she looks regular again. Old people wear funny clothes and eat cookies, but my mom don't – 'cause she's on a diet. ~Kacey, age 4.

~ * ~ * ~ * ~ * ~ * ~ * ~

… If you wear those stretchy kind of socks, and shirts with numbers on 'em, - you are definitely old. ~Kayla U., age 3.

~ * ~ * ~ * ~ * ~ * ~ * ~

… When you get sick and cough a lot you are probably old. Sometimes old people are sick and go in the hospital and have to get pacifiers in their mouth so they don't be too crabby. ~Kate, age 3.

~ * ~ * ~ * ~ * ~ * ~ * ~

… If you go to heaven, you are too old. Some old people go to the doctor every day and look like my grandma. The other ones just stay home and fix things. ~Reilly, age 7.

~ * ~ * ~ * ~ * ~ * ~ * ~

… Old people look like their bones show up. Then they have to live in a little house in a world called Alabama. But people can still go visit them if they want to. ~Riann, age 3.

~ * ~ * ~ * ~ * ~ * ~ * ~

… When you are really old you look funny and get yellow hair and red clothes. Really old people only stand up to make dinner, then they sit down, eat waffles and go to bed - 'cause old people sleep a lot! Old people kinda look like dead. ~Anna, age 3.

~ * ~ * ~ * ~ * ~ * ~ * ~

… If you are 'bout 15 and acting a fool, you can be old. Then you got to start getting a job so you can buy golden teeth, and one of them electric wheelchairs. ~DeShaun., age 3.

~ * ~ * ~ * ~ * ~ * ~ * ~

... Really old people just stay in the house and read books all day. I don't think old people are allowed to go outside. ~Nick M., age 5.

~ * ~ * ~ * ~ * ~ * ~ * ~

... Old people have just a little hair and like to wash dishes all day. They might wear glasses and look like a grandpa though, so usually they just stay in the house. ~Hayden, age 4.

~ * ~ * ~ * ~ * ~ * ~ * ~

... Really old people die. Regular old people are not dead yet - they have to get a job and fix things. And sometimes they take care of kids and play hide and go seek with them. But they don't like roller coasters though! ~Hunter H., age 5.

~ * ~ * ~ * ~ * ~ * ~ * ~

... Skinny people are usually really old. They have to make beef jerky and stuff like that to eat, and they drink lots of pop. Old people live in really old houses and eat lots of stew. Then they just go to sleep. ~Ryan, age 4.

~ * ~ * ~ * ~ * ~ * ~ * ~

... Old people can't get out of the hospital very much 'cause usually they just break a hip. Really old people drive kids crazy when they only watch news on TV, and play old people games on the computer. They can't even eat grapefruit anymore! ~Halley, age 4.

~ * ~ * ~ * ~ * ~ * ~ * ~

... Really old people are about 10 years old I think. Yeah, like my momma. Old people only go out to play in the summer. When it's freezing cold they have to stay in the house and eat chicken. ~Shane, age 4.

~ * ~ * ~ * ~ * ~ * ~ * ~

... Really old people have squishes on their face, and it's flat too. They have to push something when they walk so they don't fall down, and they hold handles in the shower. Then they eat dinner and go to bed all day until they die. ~Brendan P., age 3.

~ * ~ * ~ * ~ * ~ * ~ * ~

… If you are old you have to live on the old people street and just eat pizza and donuts and water and Coca-Cola – nothing else. Really old people don't go to work, they just love each other – like my grandpa and grandma. ~Cole, age 4.

~ * ~ * ~ * ~ * ~ * ~ * ~

… Old people are about 34 and look like my dad. Some old people wear work clothes and eat spicy pizza, but the rest of them live in Michigan, watch TV and go to bed really late. ~Connor, age 4.

~ * ~ * ~ * ~ * ~ * ~ * ~

… When you are really old you stomp, stomp, stomp when you walk. If you're just a little bit old you grow bigger and bigger and look kinda fancy and go dancing. ~Kelcie, age 3.

~ * ~ * ~ * ~ * ~ * ~ * ~

… Grown-ups are old. So are mothers. They usually eat just dinner – and nothing else. They laugh and pretend they are funny like me, but they're not. To have fun they go play with their old people friends – like dinosaurs. ~Sophia M., age 3.

~ * ~ * ~ * ~ * ~ * ~ * ~

… You know you are really old when you walk like a crazy lady and go to the store a lot. Old people need lots of food. ~Sydney B., age 5.

~ * ~ * ~ * ~ * ~ * ~ * ~

… Old people get achey-breaky and have to go to the hospital and get something put in their mouth. That's when they are 'bout 100 years old. People that are only regular old just get big, go to work and get money. ~Austin L., age 3.

~ * ~ * ~ * ~ * ~ * ~ * ~

… You can tell when somebody is old 'cause their skin is wrinkly and their throat is big and wobbly. Old people pretty much always stay at home and watch TV while they take a nap. They wear special underwear like my poppa - with the Grinch on them, and they like to drink a lot of pop. I think when you're about 95 you're really old. ~Donovan, age 8.

~ * ~ * ~ * ~ * ~ * ~ * ~

… Old people go to the grocery store a lot - but they only buy salad. ~Gillian, age 4.

~ * ~ * ~ * ~ * ~ * ~ * ~

… A person gets really old when they wear sparkly clothes, live in a big old house and don't ever go to work. They just stay home and eat lots of macaroni and cheese, and vegetables. In the summer, all the old people go to Chicago for vacation. I think my daddy is almost old, 'cause he's 35. ~Leah, age 5.

~ * ~ * ~ * ~ * ~ * ~ * ~

… Old people can be doctors, or they can be teachers. Some old people don't like to work so they just stay home and act mean. Oh, and old people always have to wear clothes when they go outside. ~Luci, age 4.

~ * ~ * ~ * ~ * ~ * ~ * ~

… If you don't have any hair and wear old shirts you are old. Old people stay at home in their wheelchairs and eat eggs and pancakes every day. They like to drink chocolate milk and orange juice too - I think it's 'cause they have worms in their bodies. ~Caleb M., age 4.

~ * ~ * ~ * ~ * ~ * ~ * ~

… Old people like to kiss you. That's all I got to say. ~Drake, age 4.

~ * ~ * ~ * ~ * ~ * ~ * ~

… Old people know how to eat hot sauce and help build houses. Really old people look like grown-ups and even sweat a little bit, but not too much. ~David W., age 3.

~ * ~ * ~ * ~ * ~ * ~ * ~

… You know old people have different faces – they turn into different colors all over and mostly look like women. Some of them eat garbage, but most of them eat lots of peas and mashed potatoes and drink Sprite. Old people have to let other people drive them around, but they don't really go anywhere. They just go for rides. ~Jacob, age 5.

~ * ~ * ~ * ~ * ~ * ~ * ~

… When you are 'bout 35 you kinda look like you are ready to go to heaven. So then you go for a ride and don't ever come home. ~Thomas, age 4.

~ * ~ * ~ * ~ * ~ * ~ * ~

… Some old people clean up their own messes. Really old people get big muscles and have big sailboats. They can play with big toys and live in old houses too, and they eat at McDonalds – a lot! ~Brenden H., age 4.

~ * ~ * ~ * ~ * ~ * ~ * ~

… When you don't have any hair - you are old. I like old people 'cause they are nice and give kids treats. ~Kyle, age 4.

~ * ~ * ~ * ~ * ~ * ~ * ~

… If you are older than me, then you are really old. Old people get to play with cash registers and pretend to be doctors if they want to. But they can only eat a little bit of waffles. ~Wes, age 4.

~ * ~ * ~ * ~ * ~ * ~ * ~

… Old people don't know much. They just play, laugh, and cry. ~Zac, age 3.

~ * ~ * ~ * ~ * ~ * ~ * ~

… Really old people live to about 40 years old. Then they ride in a wheelchair for a while. Then they lay down and wait to die. ~Lisa, age 4.

~ * ~ * ~ * ~ * ~ * ~ * ~

… Well, I know really old hands have skin that is popped up. And I know old people eat good food – not junk food - but they have to go to the dentist a lot because they have rotten teeth. Oh, and they wear beautiful dresses that are cool, and go lots of places for fun. ~Dylan O., age 4.

~ * ~ * ~ * ~ * ~ * ~ * ~

… Old people drink a lot of water, then go to the playground and fall down the slide. ~Elli, age 4.

~ * ~ * ~ * ~ * ~ * ~ * ~

… You are old when your skin is really soft but your hair isn't. Old people have white hair and purple clothes and go to Florida. Sometimes they can go outside, but only to pet the old animals. ~Jared, age 4.

~ * ~ * ~ * ~ * ~ * ~ * ~

… You are old when the candles on your birthday cake are a 3 and a 1. Really old people can be big or small. They like to take kids to school and visit with other old people. Some old people like to play in their bedrooms a lot. ~Cameron, age 4.

~ * ~ * ~ * ~ * ~ * ~ * ~

… Old people are hairy all over the place, but they are allowed to draw with pens! ~Gabrielle, age 4.

~ * ~ * ~ * ~ * ~ * ~ * ~

… When you look like my grandma - you are definitely old. Old people can play games and color with crayons all by themselves. ~Jake D., age 3.

~ * ~ * ~ * ~ * ~ * ~ * ~

… Old people have boo-boos on their arms and hands and elbows and chest. And if they are really old, they need holdy things to walk, or some have wheely things. Old people eat salad a lot. But mostly they just watch TV. ~Joseph F., age 4.

~ * ~ * ~ * ~ * ~ * ~ * ~

… I don't think old people do very much, they just sit around and play cards and eat carrots. ~Makayla, age 4.

~ * ~ * ~ * ~ * ~ * ~ * ~

… I've seen old people before. They have lumps all over their face and their hair changes colors whenever they wash it. For fun they rip all the stuff off the wall and paint it blue and pink –'cause that's their favorite colors – but then they get tired and they have to sit down and rest a lot before they go home. ~Zack, age 4.

~ * ~ * ~ * ~ * ~ * ~ * ~

… Old people drink lots of coffee, then they go brush their teeth. And they laugh silly – like Ha Ha – like that. Old people pretend they like sweaters and go in the woods to hunt bears, but they only catch rainbow fish. Old people usually like blue clothes, going shopping, and washing their hands. Old people are boring. ~Chad, age 4.

~ * ~ * ~ * ~ * ~ * ~ * ~

… When you are old you are not very strong, so you can't lift up little kids; you just have to visit with them. Some old people go to Alaska but the rest just stay home and clean the house and then go to bed. ~Jimmy, age 4.

~ * ~ * ~ * ~ * ~ * ~ * ~

… If you are really old, your skin comes up and you can't push it down again. Really old people have dirt spots on their skin and they can't wash them off – they stay on forever! When you're really old you are nice, use a wheelchair, and have a special bed. That's when you're about 100. ~Eric C., age 5.

~ * ~ * ~ * ~ * ~ * ~ * ~

… When you get old you are a little bit fat and have to wear bigger clothes. Old people love kids and like to watch soccer in real life. They also like to rake the gardens and water the plants. Then they are so tired they have to go to bed. ~Emma B., age 4.

~ * ~ * ~ * ~ * ~ * ~ * ~

… You get wrinkly skin when you get old. And white hair. Oh, and don't forget about beards, old people get beards too. Really old people don't move a lot and they need people to do stuff for them until they get to be 100. That's pretty much when they die. ~Josh, age 7.

~ * ~ * ~ * ~ * ~ * ~ * ~

… Old people always try to run away from ghosts so they don't die. But since they can't run very fast - they usually do die. ~Michael, age 4.

~ * ~ * ~ * ~ * ~ * ~ * ~

… If you are really old, they make you live somewhere else. Then you get older 'cause they don't let you go nowhere – except to take out the garbage. Old people love to take out the garbage. ~Mickayla, age 4.

~ * ~ * ~ * ~ * ~ * ~ * ~

I know old people have brains that are tired – even in the morning; maybe that's why they like to eat stuff like Sloppy Joes and broccoli. And their legs get tired if they walk too much, like a couple of miles or something, so then they have to sit down and rest. But mostly old people have problems remembering stuff. I think it's 'cause they lived so long their brains are all full and there is no more room left for new 'rememberies'. ~Quinn, age 8.

~ * ~ * ~ * ~ * ~ * ~ * ~

… Really old people look like a monster truck, only not so big. They can't *drive* monster trucks; they have to drive tractors when they go to visit the other old people's houses, but they do *look* like them. ~Ethan S., age 3.

~ * ~ * ~ * ~ * ~ * ~ * ~

… How do I know when somebody is old? It's easy, first you get wrinkles, and then you die. ~Sydney P., age 5.

~ * ~ * ~ * ~ * ~ * ~ * ~

###

A NOTE FROM THE AUTHOR

I love hearing from my readers, and I answer all my mail personally. If you enjoyed this book, would you be kind enough to leave a review on Amazon? Even if it's only a few words - it really does make a difference, and would be very much appreciated.

Simply go to www.Amazon.com and type Kristi Porter into the search bar. Then choose the appropriate story, click reviews, then click create your own review and let me know what you thought.

~ ~ ~

If you would like to receive an automatic email when my next book is released, go to http://eepurl.com/ES3kD to sign up. Your email address will never be shared and you can unsubscribe at any time.

~ ~ ~

Thanks so much for taking the time to read and review my work. It's readers like you that help make my next book even better!

Kristi Porter

OTHER BOOKS BY KRISTI PORTER
Available at Amazon.com and bookstores everywhere.

***Babies Come From... Where?!? Funny Happens When Kids Explain Pregnancy & Birth* i**s the result of hundreds of interviews with children ages three to twelve, who were simply asked "Where do you think babies come from?" and allowed to answer freely, giving as much or as little explanation as they saw fit. Now, their candid, uncensored and often hilarious answers have been collected and made available for all to enjoy in this delightful little book that is sure to be a favorite for years to come.

~ ~ ~

Priceless Proverbs - Funny Happens When Kids Finish Famous Sayings is a clever collection of words and crayon art created by children of today. Honest and raw, this small book is an utter delight as each old saying or proverb is revised and filtered through the innocent minds of children ages 3 to 12. Sayings that have become so clichéd to we adults, take on a totally new twist as children tend to tell it as it is, and you're certain to find delightful surprises on every page. Highly relatable, this book will make you want to interview the kid closest to you for even more "Priceless Proverbs!"

~ ~ ~

Priceless Proverbs - Book 2, is the second volume of the wildly popular Priceless Proverbs Collection. It features over one hundred additional quotes - wise, entertaining and uncensored - by kids ages three to twelve who were asked to finish well-known proverbs or famous sayings all on their own. Great for anyone that loves children or simply needs a smile to brighten their day.

~ ~ ~

Stranger Danger - How to Talk to Kids About Strangers is a guide to help parents and caregivers of children ages 3-8 teach kids about strangers in a fun, interactive, and age appropriate way - without scaring them. This easy to read, step by step guide gives parents age appropriate words and activities to use with even the youngest of children. Covering everything from who is a stranger, to when and how to fight back, *Stranger Danger - How to Talk to Kids About Strangers* is a must read guide for today's parents.

ABOUT THE AUTHOR

Kristi Porter has over twenty-five years of experience working with young children, both as a preschool teacher, and as an award winning child care provider. She holds a degree in Early Childhood Education and Development, as well as a national Child Development Associate Credential. In 1999, she was awarded the Governor's Quality Care Award for her outstanding commitment to the care and education of young children.

Always a reader, Kristi never thought much about writing until she entered a writing contest sponsored by the Detroit Free Press. Her story - The Worst Vacation Ever - went on to be published in a travel anthology that was distributed worldwide. This was followed by numerous articles published in local magazines and newspapers. As her love of writing grew, she added adult fiction, how-to books for parents, and short humor pieces to her repertoire.

But kids and writing aren't all Kristi relishes. She also enjoys bicycling, video games, photography, Facebook, and spending time with family. She lives in Michigan.

CONNECT WITH KRISTI ONLINE
Twitter: @KristiPorter3
Facebook: Facebook/Kristi Porter - Author
Website: http://happikamper.weebly.com
Email: Kristiporter03@gmail.com

ACKNOWLEDGEMENTS

I'd like to extend a warm thanks to Lynn Dahl Scholl, Tish Huber Winton, and Sheri Berge, for helping me conduct hundreds of interviews with children over the years. I couldn't have done it without all of you.

Many thanks as well to the White Lake Writers Group for their guidance, encouragement, and support as I sorted through all of those interviews to put this book together.

A special thanks goes out to Tirzah Goodwin, for her awesome cover design; & to my three amazing grandsons for their help with illustrations.

Lots of love, respect and appreciation to my husband for his understanding and support as I spent countless hours in front of the computer, preparing this book for publication.

And to my mom, for always believing in me, encouraging me, and pestering me to finish this and other projects - I love you more than words can say.

And finally, a heartfelt thank you to the children of North Muskegon, who allowed me into their hearts and minds, and gave me a remarkable glimpse into this wonderful world we live in - thru their eyes, their minds, and their perceptions.

Priceless.

10222295R00025

Printed in Germany
by Amazon Distribution
GmbH, Leipzig